This book is dedicated
to raising the next generation
in the light of self-love.
To those young at heart
and old in soul,
it's never too late.

Book design and illustration by Wendy Fedan, Create A Way Design & Publishing
www.CAWpublishing.com

Hardcover ISBN: 979-8-218-24489-7

Your AMAZING Body:
A Self-Love Story

Written by Änna Bencivenga

Illustrated by Wendy Fedan

...Your body is AMAZING?

From the day you are born,
you are always changing.

You start as a baby
learning so many things:

How to walk

How to
talk

NO!

How to run

Mommeeeee!

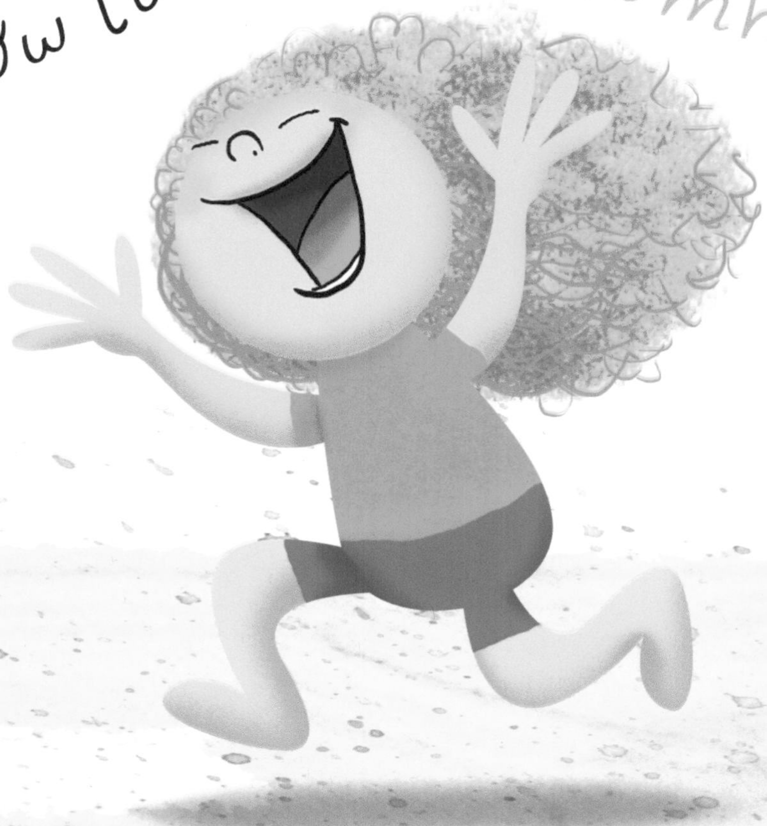

How to sing

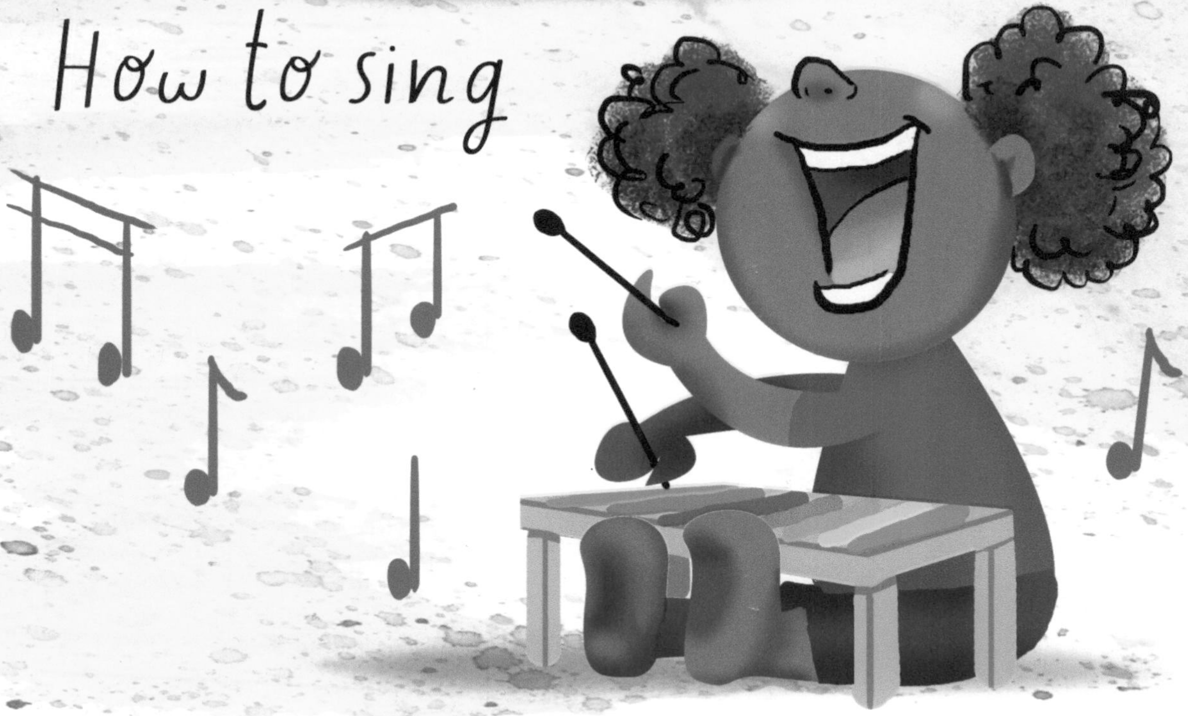

But while all of this is happening your body just DOES some incredible things!

Your ears: they HEAR

Your arms: they hug.

Your lungs: they breathe.

Your mouth: it eats.

Your heart: it pumps blood

Your hair: it grows...

...and you may want it cut.

Every BODY is different
and that's great, too.

You will get older and smarter trying many new things...

...but one thing is with you through all of the change.

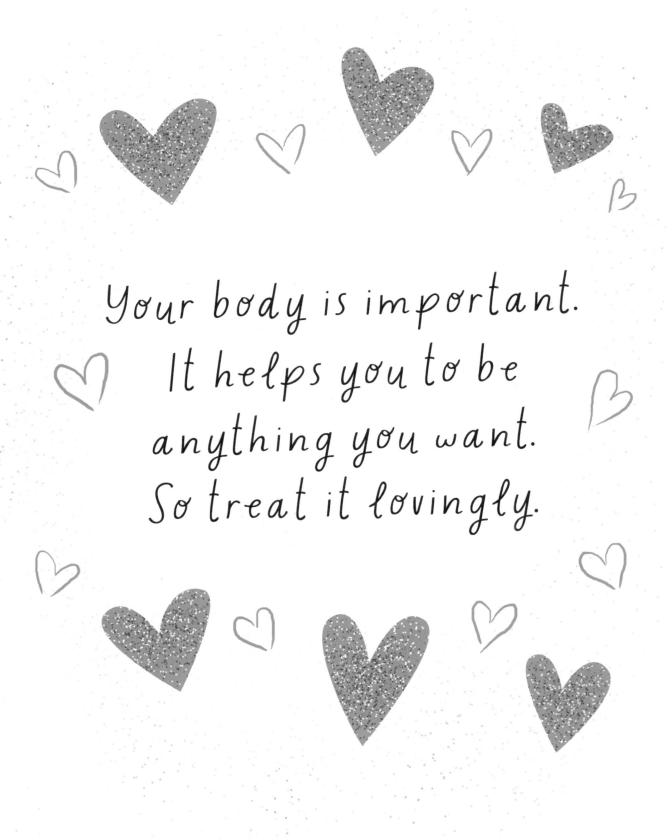

Your body is important.
It helps you to be
anything you want.
So treat it lovingly.

Feed it good food.

Don't forget your veggies!

MOVE iT

to stay strong

and feel healthy!

Sleep is important.
It lets your body heal.

Remember
to brush
your teeth
after every
single meal.

Your body will change.

But it is also the one thing
that will always see you through.

Through the good times
and the tough times
don't forget this one thing:

always treat it
with kindness,
love and respect.

Because your body is
AMAZING.